al·pha·bet [al-fuh-bet, -bit] —noun

1. the letters of a language in their customary order.
2. any system of characters or signs with which a language is written: the Greek alphabet.
3. any such system for representing the sounds of a language: the phonetic alphabet.
4. first elements; basic facts; simplest rudiments: the alphabet of genetics.

the alphabet, a system of writing, developed in the ancient Near East and transmitted from the northwest Semites to the Greeks, in which each symbol ideally represents one sound unit in the spoken language, and from which most alphabetical scripts are derived. [Origin: 1375–1425; late ME alphabete < LL alphabétum, alter. of Gk alphábétos. See alpha, beta]

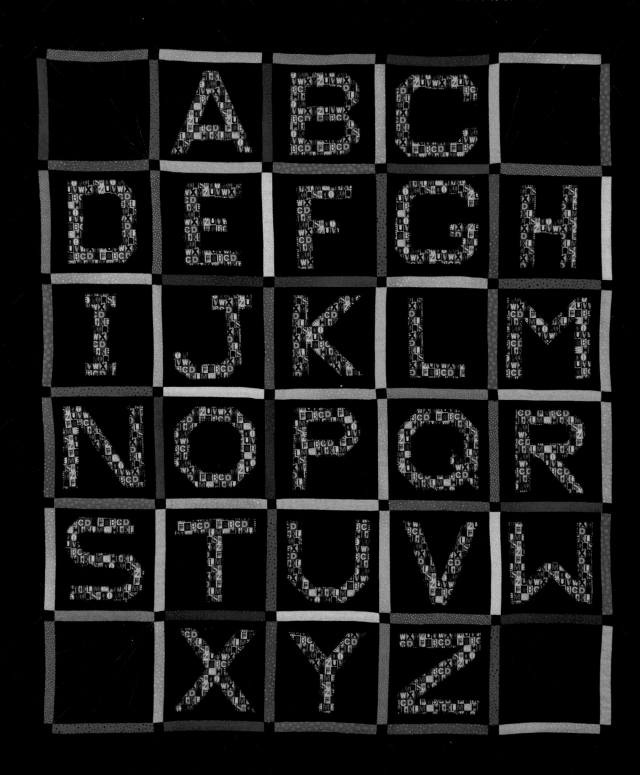

Alphabet Quilts
Letters for All Ages

By Bea Oglesby

Alphabet Quilts
Letters for All Ages
By Bea Oglesby

Editor: Deb Rowden
Technical Editor: Barbara Nesemeyer
Designer: Kelly Ludwig, Ludwig Design
Photography: Aaron T. Leimkuehler
Illustration: Eric Sears, Gary Embrey Design
Original artwork: Lon Eric Craven
Production assistance: Jo Ann Groves

Published by:
Kansas City Star Books
1729 Grand Blvd.
Kansas City, Missouri, USA 64108

First edition, first printing
ISBN: 978-1-933466-26-2

Library of Congress Control Number: 2006940946

Printed in the United States of America by Walsworth
Publishing Co., Marceline, MO

KANSAS CITY STAR BOOKS

To order copies, call StarInfo at (816) 234-
4636 and say "Books."

PickleDish.com

The Quilter's Home Page www.PickleDish.com

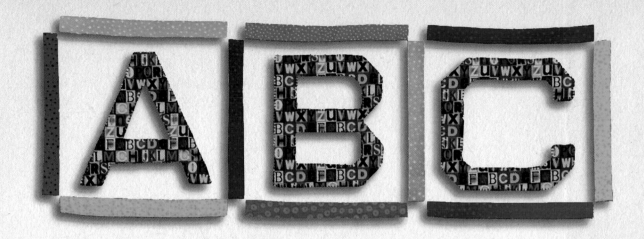

Table of Contents

Dedication

To my ten great-grandchildren: Sam, Katie and Henry Watson; Nicholas, Michael and Lauren Zarras; Serena, Olivia and Daniel Schiller; and Lillie Thomasset, with the hope that the alphabet will always be a part of their lives and instill in them the love of words and books.

Acknowledgements

To—

My husband and my three daughters who give me the support needed to continue my work.

My grandchildren, who all have asked me to make an alphabet quilt. It was because of them that I started working on alphabets.

My friends at the Johnson County Resource Library, who have all assisted me in the research of my projects.

My friends at the local quilt shops: Carol Kirchhoff at Prairie Point, Debbie Richards at Quilters Haven and Elaine Johnson at Harper's Fabric and Quilt Company. It is such a pleasure to get your feedback and advice on fabrics and colors.

My many students who have taken my classes. I hope that I have made a difference in your life as you have made a difference in my life with your enthusiasm and eagerness.

My editor, Deb Rowden, who is not only my editor, but who has become a good friend. Thank you for your patience, support, time and for listening.

Finally, my thanks to Doug Weaver, Edie McGinnis and everyone at Kansas City Star Books for their continued support. It has been a pleasure to know and to work with you.

About the Author

Bea has been a quiltmaker, teacher and lecturer since 1990. Because of her love of nature, flowers and art, she has found a never-ending source of ideas for appliqué, her favorite medium. As a result, most of her work is in appliqué. She created this alphabet book because of her love of books, and her study of the many different styles of the alphabet. This led Bea to combine designs with letters. Bea teaches and lectures in the Kansas City area and belongs to several local quilt guilds. She volunteers weekly at the Johnson County Resource Library. Bea lives in Overland Park, Kansas with her husband Red. She wrote her first book in 1999 and has completed a book every year since. Her first Kansas City Star book, *Art Nouveau Quilts for the 21st Century*, was published in 2006.

An Introduction to Alphabets

Latin scripts were developed over 2,000 years ago, but the alphabet that we use today was acquired from the Etruscans by the Romans. It had 21 letters. The Romans added the Greek letters Y and Z and during the medieval period the letters J, U and W were added for phonetic values to bring the number of letters up to our current alphabet of 26.

There are numerous type design styles, from the Renaissance and the formal script of the Vatican to many modern interpretations. Many of the modern interpretations had their origins in the advertising industry. These typefaces can be whimsical, formal, elegant or free style. The script was often made to fit the page and the letters themselves developed from the pen or brush that was used.

I offer a basic reference and patterns for lettering to be used in quiltmaking. While searching through antique quilts, I found many nineteenth century quilts had the alphabet on them, possibly used by mothers while crossing the prairie by wagon train to teach their children.

I have made quilts featuring four different alphabets.
- The block alphabet (Chapter 1) can be used as just plain letters or as a child's quilt with an animal for each of the letters.
- The cursive alphabet (Chapter 2) has both upper and lower case letters.
- The floral alphabet (Chapter 3) features large letters with a flower for each letter.
- Finally, there is the Spencerian alphabet (Chapter 4), which is also known as Roundhand. This classy script was developed by Platt Rogers Spencer in the nineteenth century. Our modern script is developed from it.

Letters in these alphabet quilts can by appliquéd by hand or machine, or they can be appliquéd with fusible web. I have used both methods to create these quilts.

These letters present endless possibilities. A single letter can be used for a pillow or small wallhanging. The letters can also be reduced in size to place a name or message on a quilt. These alphabets can be used in various sizes for wallhangings or crib quilts. The quilts can also be made larger with the addition of borders. I took some liberties in adapting the letters for fabric appliqué. See the Gallery on page 118 for more ideas.

Choose what letters or alphabet that you would like to use—be creative and make it your own.

Alphabet Basic Instructions

Read these instructions before beginning any of the projects. Use 1/4" seam allowances.

Some of these quilts were appliquéd and quilted by hand and some were appliquéd using fusible web. All of these quilts can be made using either of these methods.

The smaller quilts with the block and the cursive letters are relatively simple. Choose your colors, position the letters and sew, either by hand or by using fusible web with machine edging.

The floral alphabet is a bit more challenging as each letter has a flower entwining the letter. This again is not too difficult as each letter block is individual. I made mine using fusible web, edged with a decorative stitch. I made one letter using the needleturn method (see Gallery on page 118) to prove to myself that this can be done by hand.

I made the Spencerian alphabet quilts both by needleturn and also with the fusible web. I was not sure that needleturn would work with the skinny scrolls, but following the numerical sequence, it worked.

Feel free to use the patterns with any stitching method. The choice is yours.

Fabric Preparation

I used 100 % cotton fabric in all these quilts. It is basically the fabric of choice for quilters. Thoroughly wash and rinse all fabrics. Remove the fabrics from the dryer before they are completely dry and iron them with a steam iron. This will remove sizing in the fabric and will contend with any bleeding that may occur. Fabric preparation is the same for hand appliqué and for fusible web.

Fusible Web Method

There are many fusible web brands on the market. I have used several of them and they basically all work. The important thing to remember is to follow the manufacturer's instructions for iron temperatures, time required and procedures for each brand.

When using fusible web, to avoid a backward design, the pattern must be reversed. In doing the alphabets, you may not need to reverse some of the block letters such as the A, I, or O, but it is necessary with most of the letters (such as the C, R, or S). Cursive letters should all be reversed as they are not square. The animals need not be reversed unless you want them to face a certain way. The floral alphabet letters must be reversed as the flowers entwine each letter.

Study the letters in the quilt that you plan to make before you begin. To reverse a pattern, you may be able to see through the paper pattern on the backside. If this is possible, use a permanent marker with a fine point and trace on to the back side. If it is not possible to see, use a light box or window to trace a reverse pattern.

- Copy the alphabet patterns onto the smooth side of the fusible web. Cut out each letter on the line and place this web template onto the back or the wrong side of the desired fabric. Fuse for about 5 seconds, or as long as your web brand recommends. This allows the web pattern to adhere to the fabric without melting the glue.
- If the pattern you are using is on an individual block, each letter can be fused individually. It the pattern is on full background, such as the cursive alphabet or the Spencerian alphabet, arrange all the letters and figures before any fusing is done.
- When you are happy with the arrangement, carefully peel off the paper backing and fuse the shape in place. Use a dry iron and fuse for about 10 to 15 seconds. This is long enough to melt the glue and fix the letter permanently.
- Use a narrow zigzag or a decorative machine stitch on the edge of the appliqué. This gives the appliqué a finished look. I use a machine buttonhole stitch with cotton #40 or #30 thread. This thread is heavier than regular sewing thread and covers the raw edge nicely. Sometimes I use the same color as the appliqué, and sometimes a contrast color. Experiment and decide what look you wish to have on your quilt.

Hand Appliqué

- After the background fabric is washed and ironed, I gently spray this background with starch. This gives the fabric body and makes it easier to mark. Place the fabric over the pattern and mark with a fine washout pen, a quilter's marking pencil or a chalk pencil with a fine point.
- Draw the pattern onto the dull side of freezer paper, mark the piece with its number and cut out on the pattern line.
- Position the pattern on the right side of your desired fabric and iron in place.
- Mark around each pattern with a fine point marker. This is your sewing line.
- Cut out the individual pieces leaving a 1/4" seam allowance around each piece. This may be trimmed narrower as you appliqué each individual piece.
- Turn the seam allowance to the back of each individual piece before the freezer paper is removed and crease with your thumb and finger. With cotton fabric, this gives a crease on the seam allowance for easier needleturn.
- All the appliqué pieces are numbered. Start with piece number 1 and work in sequence. Remove the freezer paper, position the piece in place and needleturn with small appliqué stitches with thread that matches the appliqué on the marked sewing line.
- After the piece has been appliquéd, wash out any markings that may show before pressing.

Finishing

Follow the tips and instructions for the finishing with each individual quilt.

Animal Alphabet

40" x 48"

For this quilt, animals join their respective block letters, playfully arranged on a background fabric.

Cutting and Assembly

- Cut the background fabric 32" x 40". This will be trimmed to size after the animals and letters are fused onto the background and the decorative edging is finished.
- Follow the basic instructions for applying the letters and the animals using fusible web (see page 6).
- Before you fuse any of the letters and animals in place, match the animal with their appropriate letter, placing some over and some under the letter. Arrange them on the background fabric and when the arrangement is pleasing, fuse the letter and animal in place. Stitch around each letter and animal for a finished look. I used #30 weight cotton thread the color of the background fabric.

Finishing

- After the letters and animals are all fused and stitched in place, press the background and trim it to the correct size of 30 1/2" x 38 1/2".
- Cut 2 strips of the inner border fabric 1 1/2" x 38 1/2" and sew to the sides.
- Cut 2 strips of the inner border fabric 1 1/2" x 32 1/2" and sew to the top and bottom.
- Cut 2 strips of the outer border fabric 4 1/2" x 40 1/2" and sew to the sides.
- Cut 2 strips of the outer border fabric 4 1/2" x 40 1/2" and sew to the top and bottom.
- Mark the quilting design you desire and layer the top, batting and backing. Pin in place about every 4" and quilt by machine.
- Bind with the outer border fabric.

Fabric Requirements

- Background – 1 1/2 yards
- Alphabet, outer border and binding – 2 yards
- Inner border – 1/4 yard
- Animals – fat quarters or bright scraps
- Fusible web – 2 yards of lightweight fusible web

Block Alphabet

34" x 39 1/2"

This cheerful child's alphabet quilt features 4" block letters on 5" squares with colorful sashing.

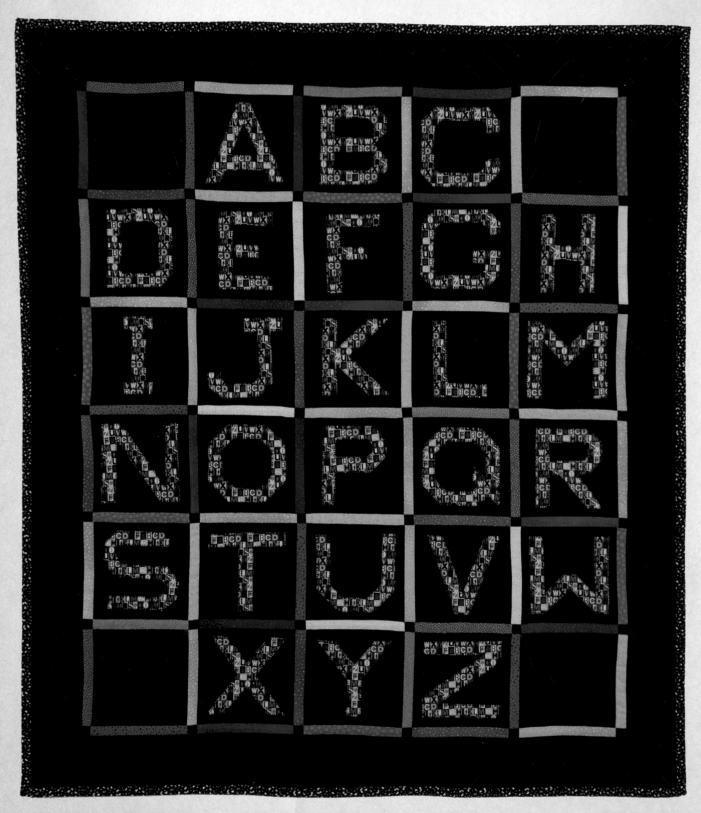

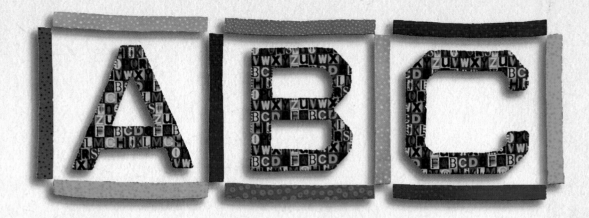

Fabric Requirements

- Background – 1 1/2 yards
- Alphabet – 1 yard
- Sashing – assorted bright scraps
- Binding – 1/2 yard
- Fusible web – 1 1/2 yards of lightweight fusible web

Cutting and Assembly

- Cut 30-5 1/2" squares from the background fabric for the alphabet and for the 4 corners.
- Follow the basic instructions for applying the letters using fusible web (see page 6).
- Fuse the letters on 26 of the background squares. Leave 4 squares blank for the 4 corners. Use a decorative stitch around each of the letters for a finished look.
- Cut 71 sashing strips 1" x 5 1/2" of assorted fabrics. Sew 2 of these sashing strips onto the sides of the alphabet letter blocks and the sides of the corner blocks.
- Sew these 6 horizontal rows with the side sashings together.

- Cut 42-1" squares of the background fabric to be used as the posts between the sashes. Sew these squares onto the remaining horizontal sashing strips.
- Sew the horizontal sashing rows onto the top and bottom of each row with the letters.
- Cut the borders 3" wide for a finished 2 1/2" border. Sew them onto all 4 sides.

Finishing

- Mark the quilting design you desire and layer the top, batting and backing. Pin in place about every 4" and quilt by machine. I used a variegated thread for color and contrast on the black background.
- Bind with a finished 1/2" border. To make this, cut the binding fabric 4" wide. Fold it in half with wrong sides together and press. With the raw edges matching, sew this binding onto the right side of the quilt with a 1/2" seam allowance. Turn it to the back of the quilt and slipstitch in place.

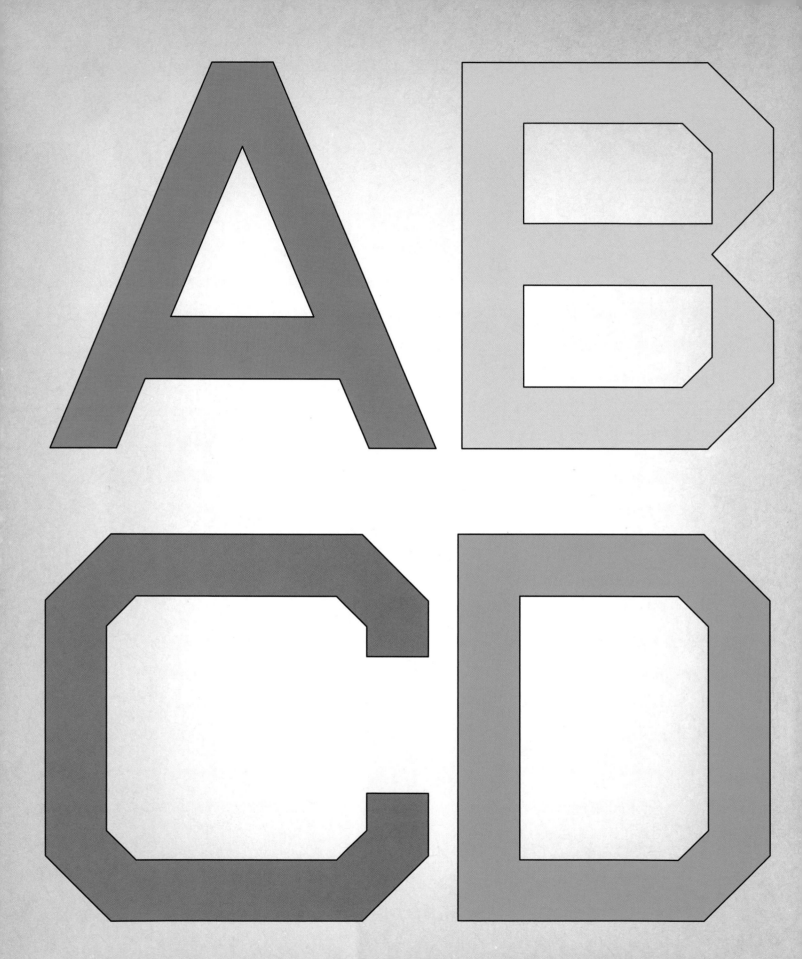

EFI

GH

Bat

Camel

Alligator

Duck

Elephant

Frog

Giraffe

Hippopotamus

Iguana

Jaguar

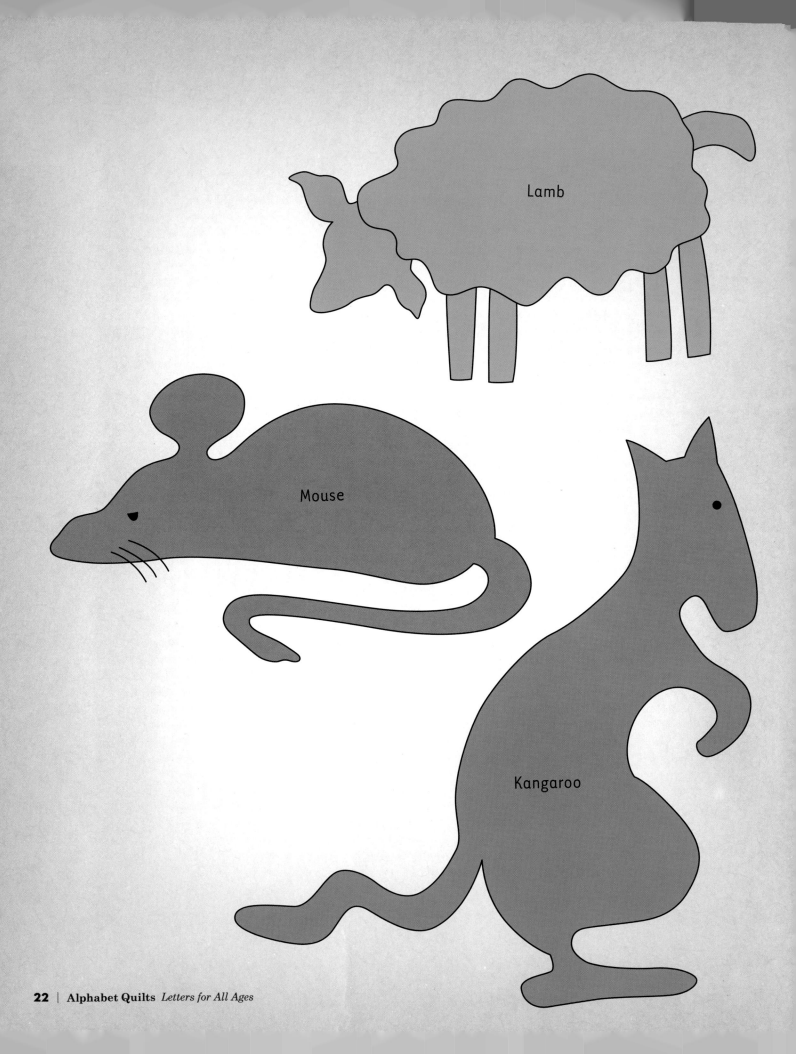

Lamb

Mouse

Kangaroo

Pig

Rabbit

Ostrich

Turtle

Quail

Swan

eXtinct

Newt

Unicorn

Zebra

Yak

Cursive Alphabet

32" x 43"

This bright and lively wallhanging or baby quilt using upper- and lower-case cursive letters is edged with 2" prairie points.

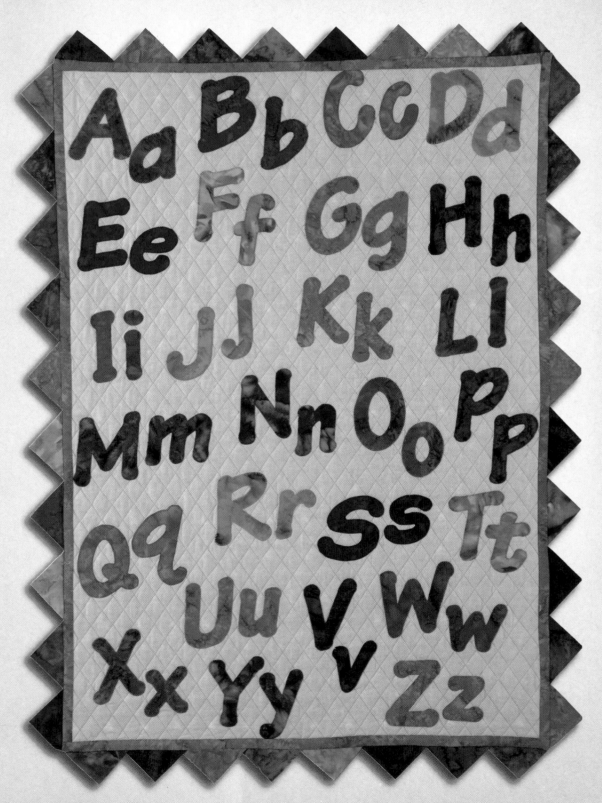

Fabric Requirements
- Background fabric – 1 1/4 yards
- Letters and prairie points – 1 1/2 yards total amount of your color choices
- Binding — 1/2 yard
- Fusible web – 1 yard

Cutting and Assembly
- Cut the background fabric 29" x 40". This will be trimmed to size after the letters are fused and stitched in place.
- Follow the basic instructions for applying the letters using fusible web (see page 6).
- Before you fuse any of the letters in place, position the total alphabet onto the background to be sure the arrangement is pleasing. When all the letters are in position, fuse them in place and stitch around each letter (I used a blanket stitch, using #30 weight thread the color of each letter) for a finished look.
- Sandwich the top, batting and backing and machine quilt the background.
- Block and trim the background to the finished size of 28 1/2" x 39 1/2".

To make Prairie Points
- Cut 36 - 5" squares from your fabric choices (see Fig. 1). Fold these squares in half diagonally (see Fig. 2), then fold them in half again and press (see Fig. 3).
- Working from the back side of the quilt, position 10 prairie points on each side and 8 on the top and bottom. Line up the raw edges of the prairie points with the raw edges of the back side of the quilt. Have all the folds of the points facing the same way and overlap each point onto the next about 1/8" to 1/4". The 2 points at the corners should just meet and form a miter.
- Stitch these points to the back of the quilt using a 1/4" seam allowance. Press the points to the outside. The raw edge will be on the front of the quilt.

Finishing

- For the binding to cover the raw edge, cut 2 strips 1" x 39 1/2" and sew to the sides. Cut 2 strips 1" x 28 1/2" and sew to the top and bottom. Slip-stitch in place to cover the raw edges. This makes a 1/2" finished binding.

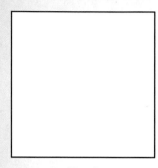

Fig. 1

- Cut a 5" square for each prairie point.

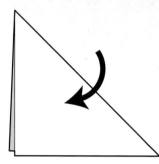

Fig. 2

- Fold in half diagonally (wrong sides together) and press.

Fig. 3

- Fold in half again and press.

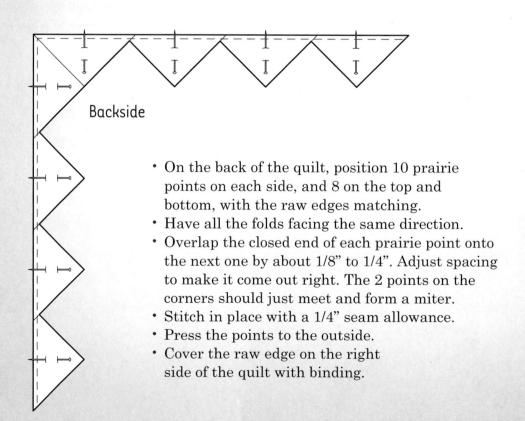

Backside

- On the back of the quilt, position 10 prairie points on each side, and 8 on the top and bottom, with the raw edges matching.
- Have all the folds facing the same direction.
- Overlap the closed end of each prairie point onto the next one by about 1/8" to 1/4". Adjust spacing to make it come out right. The 2 points on the corners should just meet and form a miter.
- Stitch in place with a 1/4" seam allowance.
- Press the points to the outside.
- Cover the raw edge on the right side of the quilt with binding.

Alphabet and Numbers

38" x 43"

Upper case cursive letters, numbers and objects for each letter
decorate this child's quilt on a pieced background.

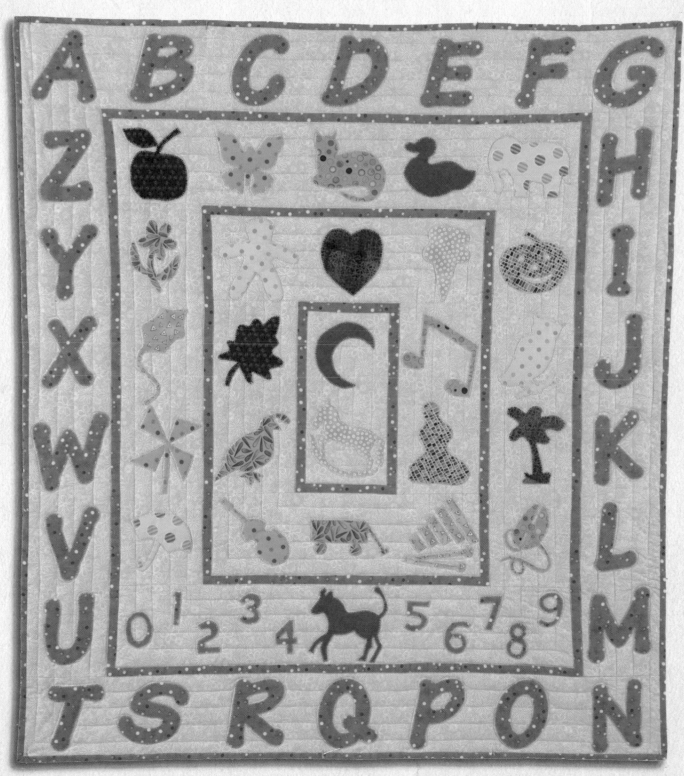

Fabric Requirements
- Background – 2 yards
- Alphabet, sashing, and binding – 1 1/2 yards
- Objects – scraps of bright colors
- Fusible web – 2 1/2 yards

Piece the Background Fabric
- Cut the sashing strips 1" wide for a 1/2" finished sash. If you use the cross grain of 40" fabric, 7 - 1" strips will be ample.
- For the background, add seam allowances to all pieces. Start with the center block and work to the outer borders (see Assembly Diagram).
- Cut 1 center block 5" x 10".
- Sash the 2 sides, top and bottom.
- Border 1: Cut from the background fabric 2 pieces 5" x 11" and sew to the sides. Cut 2 pieces 5" x 16" and sew to the top and bottom.
- Add sashing to the 2 sides and the top and bottom.
- Border 2: Cut from the background fabric 2 pieces 5" x 22" and sew to the sides. Cut 2 pieces 5" x 27" and sew to the top and bottom.
- Add sashing to the sides, top, and bottom.
- Outer or Alphabet Border: Cut from the background fabric 2 pieces 5" x 33" and sew to the sides. Cut 2 pieces 5" x 38" and sew to the top and bottom.

Assembly
- Follow the basic instructions for applying the letters, numbers and objects using the fusible web.
- Before you fuse any of the letters and objects in place, position them on the background to be sure they are spaced properly and the overall design is pleasing to the eye. When all are in position, fuse in place and stitch around each letter and object for a finished look. I used #30 weight thread the color of the background to make the blanket stitch.

Finishing
- Sandwich the top, batting and backing and machine quilt the background.
- Block and trim to size and bind with the sashing fabric.

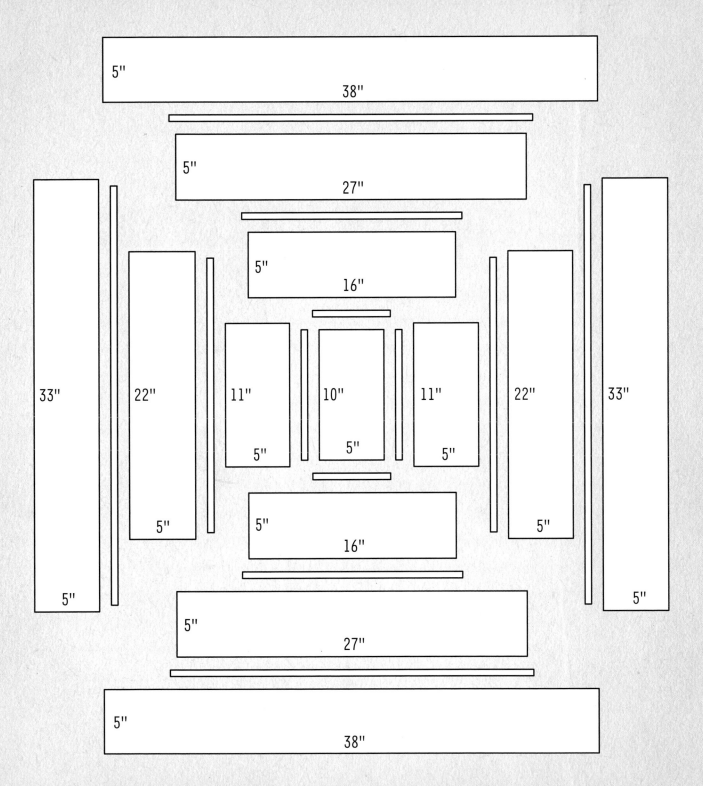

Note: these are finished sizes. Add 1/4" seam allowance to these measurements. All narrow strips are 1" wide.

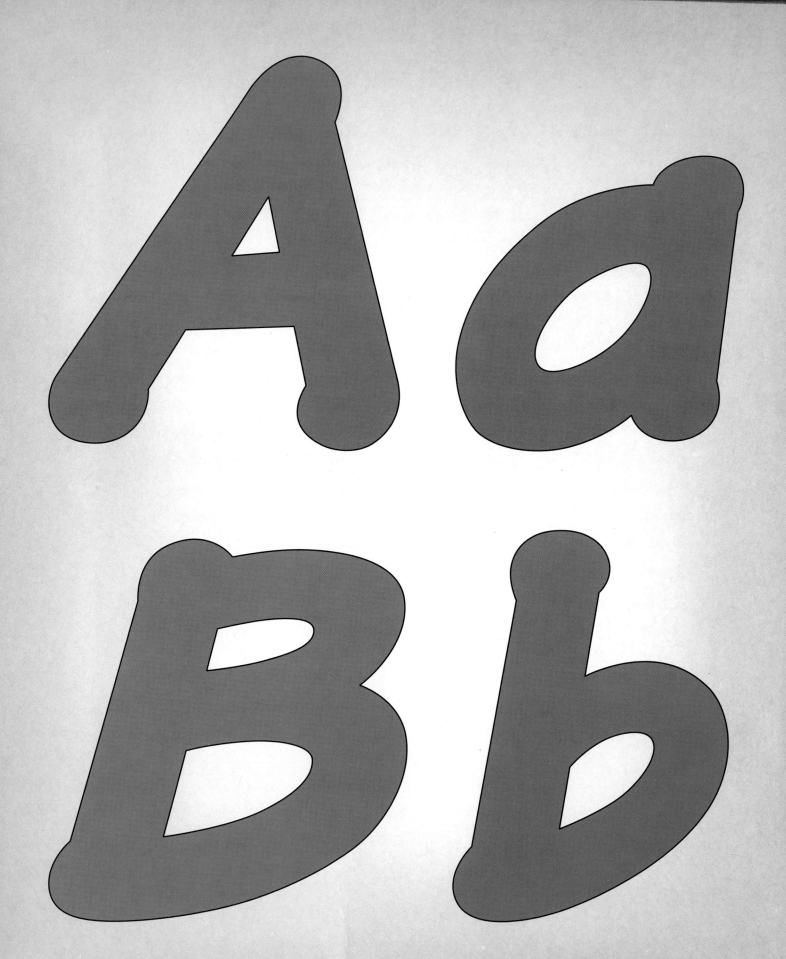

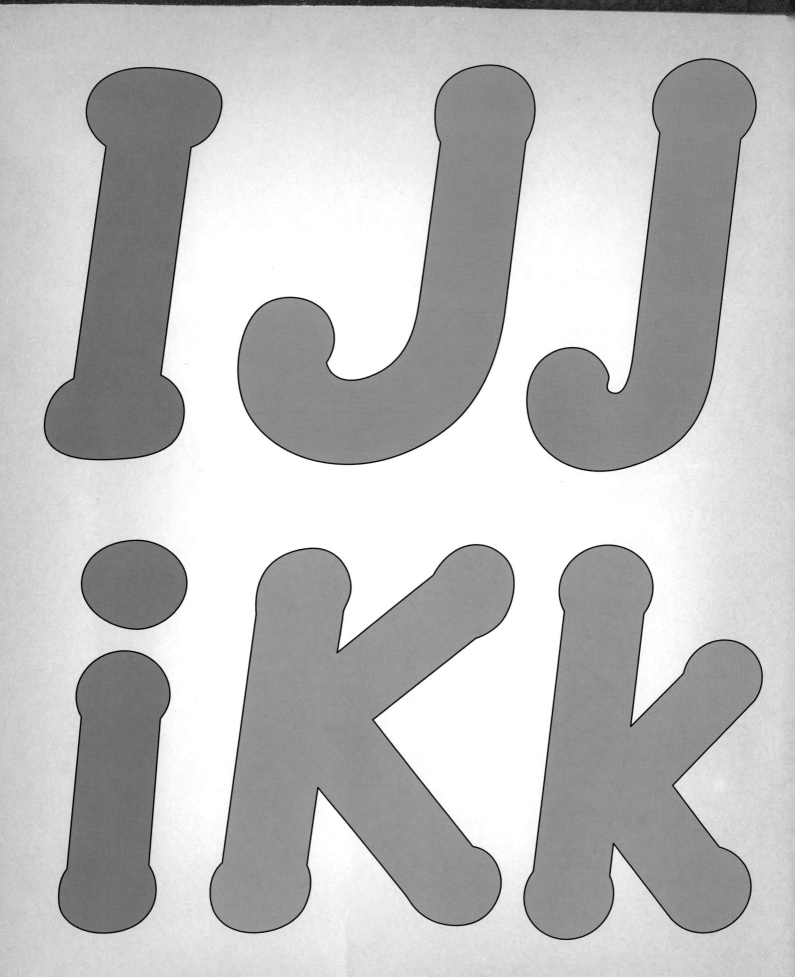

L M
l m

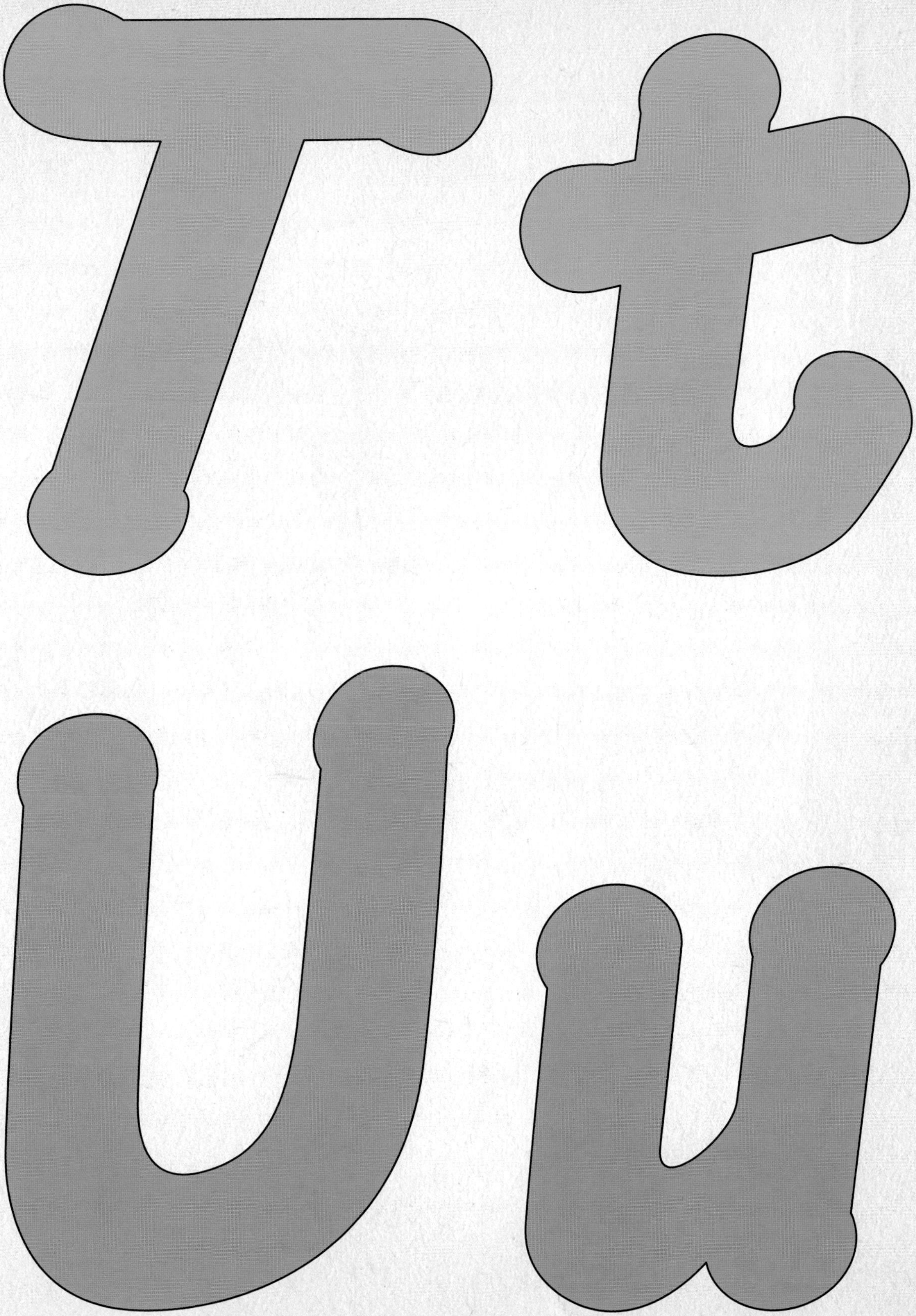

Z z

1 2 3 4 5

6 7 8 9 0

Apple

Butterfly

Cat

Duck

Elephant

Heart

Flower

Gingerbread Man

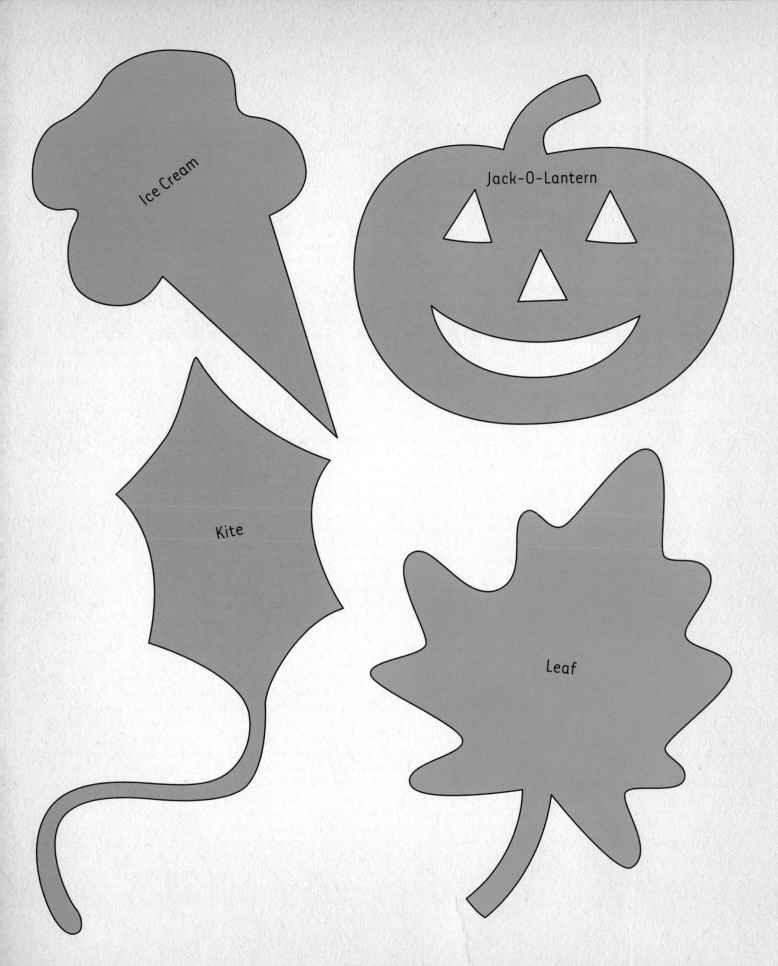

Ice Cream

Jack-O-Lantern

Kite

Leaf

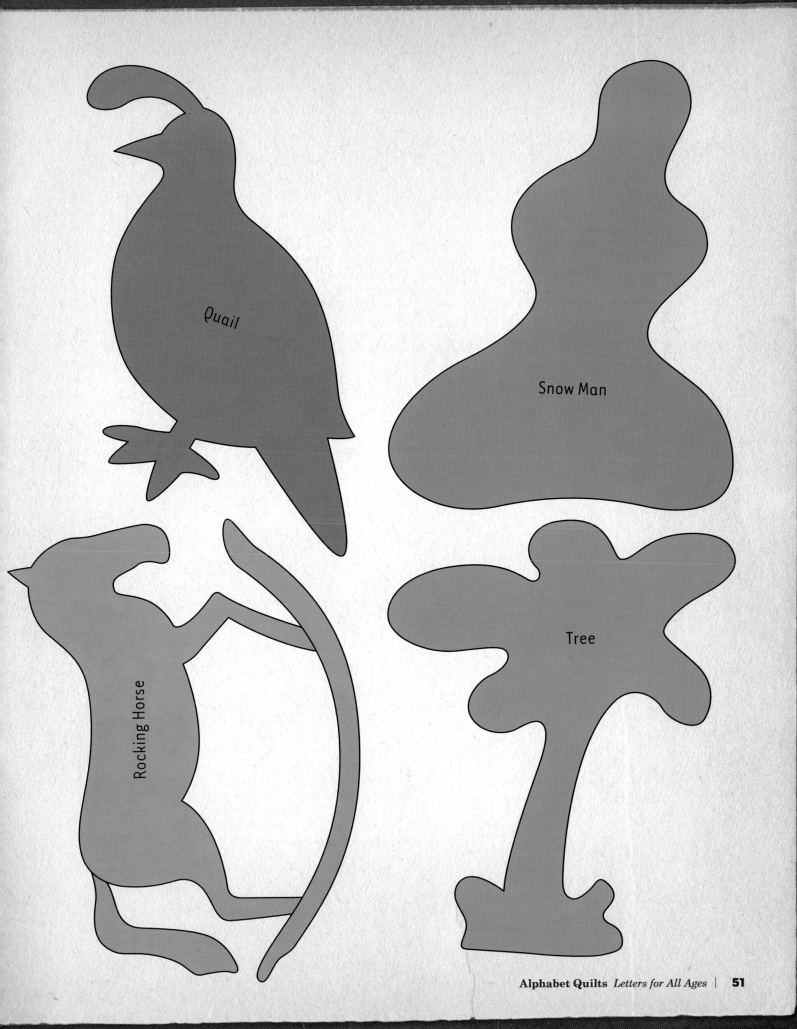

Quail

Snow Man

Rocking Horse

Tree

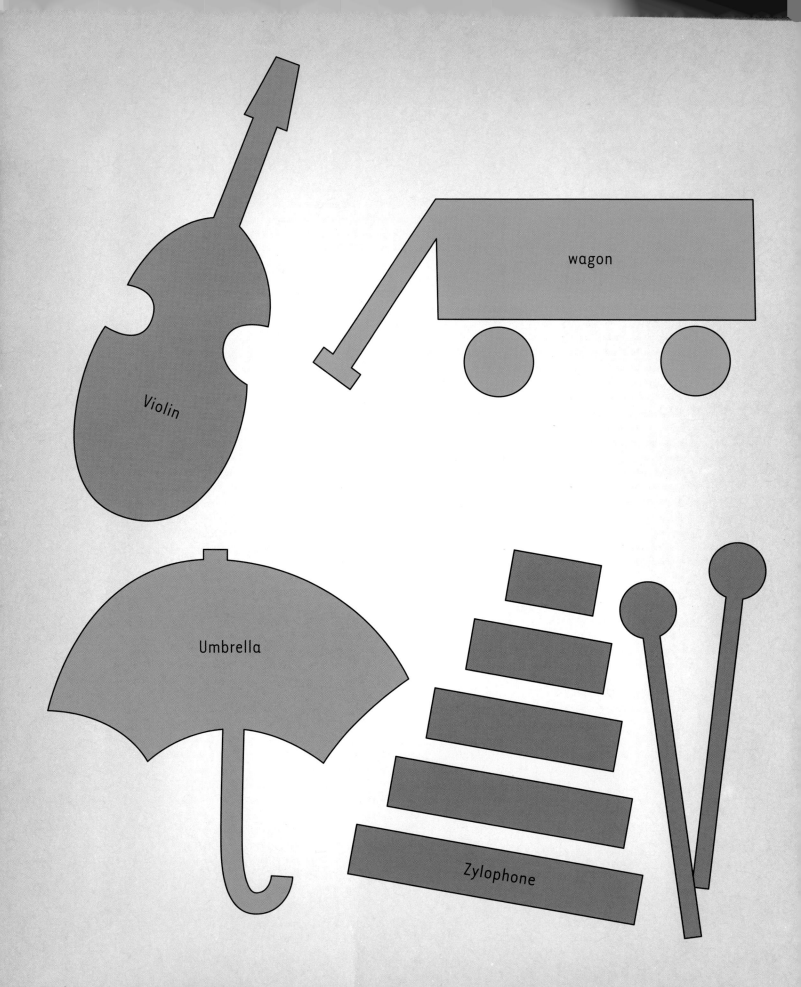

wagon

Violin

Umbrella

Zylophone

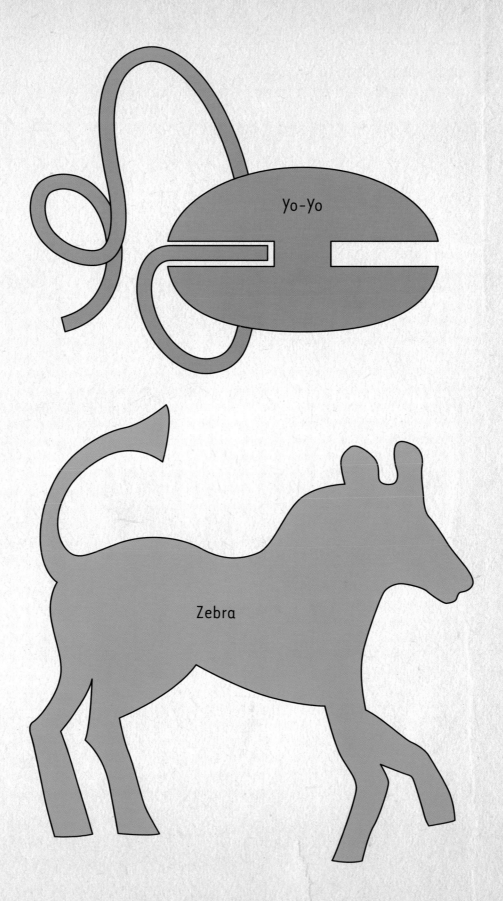

Yo-Yo

Zebra

Floral Alphabet

52" x 60"

This quilt features large block letters with a flower for each of the letters.

A Note about Letter Sizes

There are 4 different sizes of letters in this quilt—8", 9", 10" and 12". They may be arranged in any manner that you desire as long as all 5 vertical rows add up to 48". You may substitute any 8" letter with any other 8" letter or any 10" letter for any other 10" letter and these letters can be moved about in their vertical rows as long as the inches add up to 48. I started with the "A" in the top left corner, ended with "Z" in the bottom right corner and filled in with the other letters. Move the letters around and have fun.

Fabric Requirements

- Background – 2 yards
- Letters and inner border – 1 1/2 yards
- Middle border – 1/2 yard
- Outer border and binding – 1 3/4 yards
- Fusible web – 2 1/2 yards of lightweight fusible web
- Flowers and leaves – fat quarter or scraps of your choice of colors for the flowers and a minimum of 6 shades of greens; light, medium and dark for the leaves

Cutting and Assembly

Cut the background blocks for the letters as follows:
- 13 blocks 9" x 9"
- 2 blocks 9" x 10"
- 7 blocks 9" x 11"
- 4 blocks 9" x 13"
- These blocks are cut 1" larger than the finished block as some appliqué takes up more fabric than others. After the appliqué is complete, they will be trimmed to the correct size with seam allowances added.
- Place the correct size block over the pattern and mark.
- Follow the basic instructions for fusible web appliqué. Work 1 block at a time and arrange the letter, the flowers and the leaves on the background before they are fused in place. There are only 10 pieces in the "L" block, but there are 74 pieces in the "X" block. Study the pattern carefully and follow the sequence of numbers. Arrange several pieces at

a time to be certain that the ends of the leaves and flower petals will underlay the stems or the letter as shown. For a finished look, I used the blanket stitch and #30 weight thread, matching the color of the letters and the flowers. Note: Many of the blocks are embellished with embroidery (see individual patterns).

Finishing

- After the appliqué is finished, cut the blocks to their correct sizes. Be sure to add seam allowance to these blocks. Arrange in vertical rows in the design of your choice, making sure that all the rows add up to 48". Sew the blocks together in vertical rows and sew the rows together.
- Press and block the quilt to 40" x 48" plus seam allowance.
- Cut the inner border 1" wide for a finished 1/2" inner border.
- Cut the middle border 2 1/2" wide for a finished 2" middle border.
- Cut the outer border 4" wide for a finished 3 1/2" outer border.
- After the piece is finished, bind it with the outer border fabric.

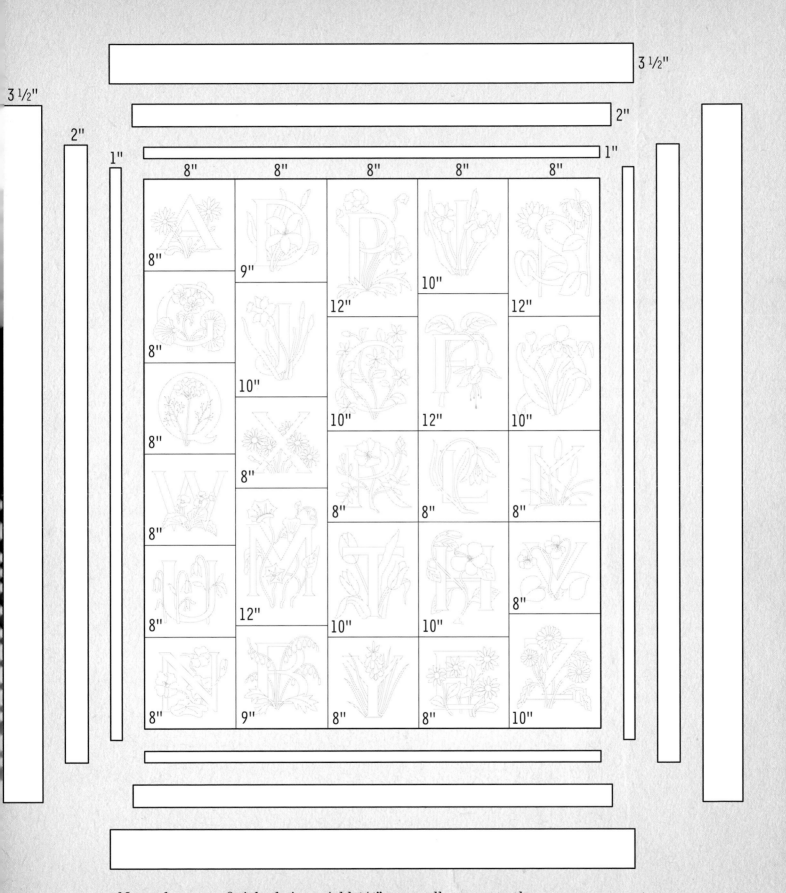

Note: these are finished sizes. Add 1/4" seam allowance to these measurements.

Aster
39 pieces

Bleeding Heart
31 pieces

Clematis
47 pieces

Daylily
16 pieces

English Daisy
57 pieces

Fuschia
16 pieces

Geranium
26 pieces

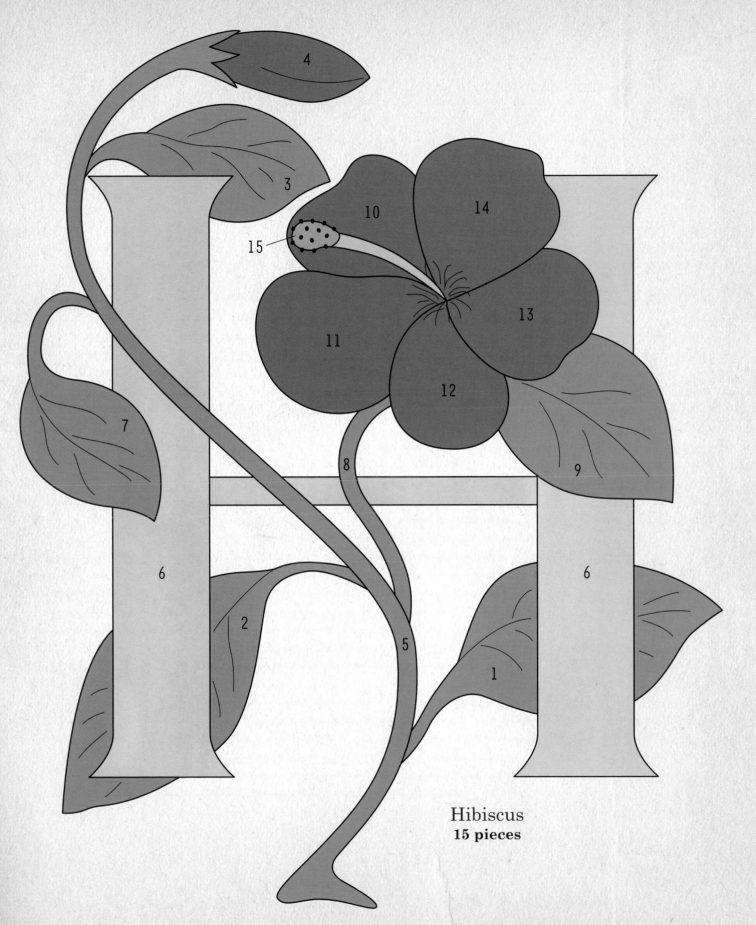

Hibiscus
15 pieces

Iris
26 pieces

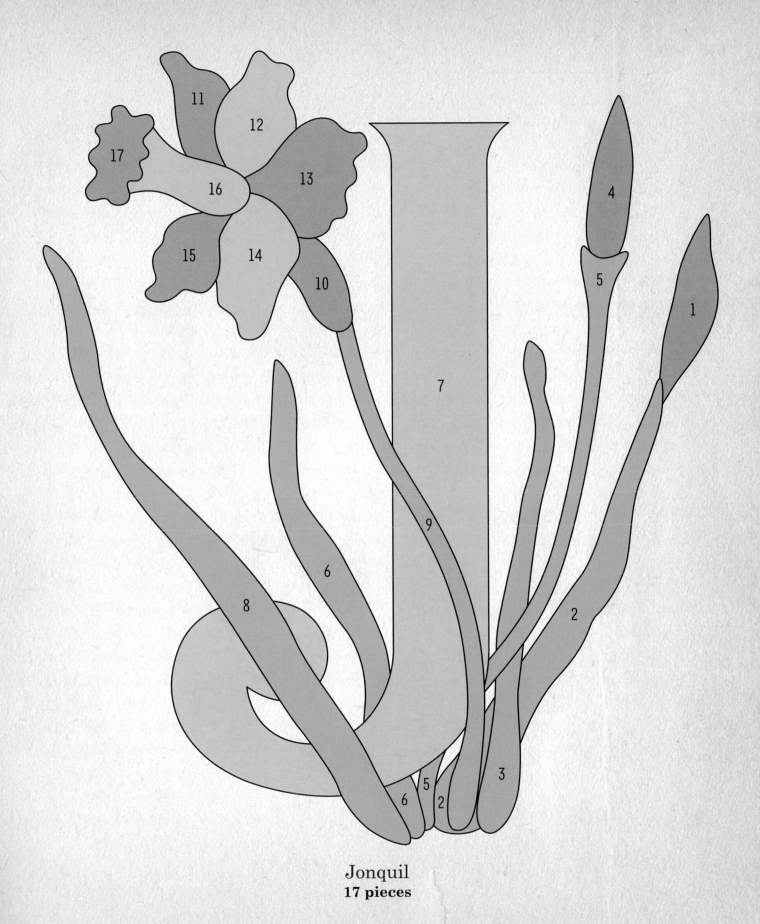

Jonquil
17 pieces

Kniphofia (Poker Plant)
13 pieces

Lily
10 pieces

Morning Glory
22 pieces

Nasturtium
23 pieces

Orchid
20 pieces

Poppy
20 pieces

Queen Anne's Lace
5 pieces

Rose
32 pieces

Sunflower
44 pieces

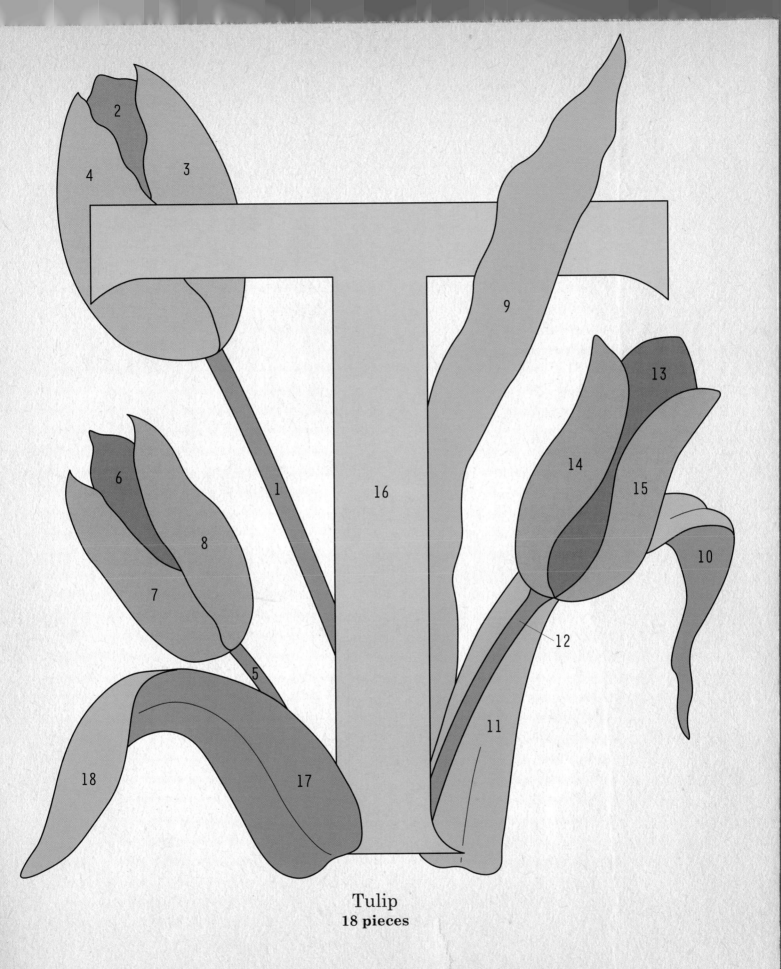

Tulip
18 pieces

Uvularia (Merry Bells)
21 pieces

Viola
17 pieces

Wax Begonia
29 pieces

Xeranthemum
74 pieces

Yucca
24 pieces

Zinnia
63 pieces

Spencerian Alphabet

46" x 56"

This two-color quilt uses Spencerian script letters on a solid background with wide borders and inside rounded corners. This is a classic script, used for formal invitations, greeting cards, and whenever a sophisticated look is desired.

Fabric Requirements
- Background – 1 1/2 yards
- Border, binding and letters – 2 1/2 yards

Cutting and Arrangement
- Cut background fabric 37" x 48". This will be trimmed to the inside measurement of 35" x 46" plus seam allowances after the appliqué is finished.
- Before you appliqué any of these letters on to the background, make a rough sketch of each of the letters and position these letters on to the background. This will insure a pleasing arrangement for the alphabet. With a washout marker, mark the place on the background for each of the letters. This is not the pattern, but the position for these letters. Leave these marks in place while you appliqué the individual letters. This is your insurance that the finished letters will be in the desired place. These marks will be washed out after the appliqué is completely finished.
- Follow the instructions for hand appliqué (see page 7) and follow the numbered sequence for each letter. There are a few letters with 4 pieces, but most have only 2 and 3 pieces in the appliqué. On some of the narrow scrolls, trim the seam allowance a bit narrower than 1/4" to eliminate bulk.

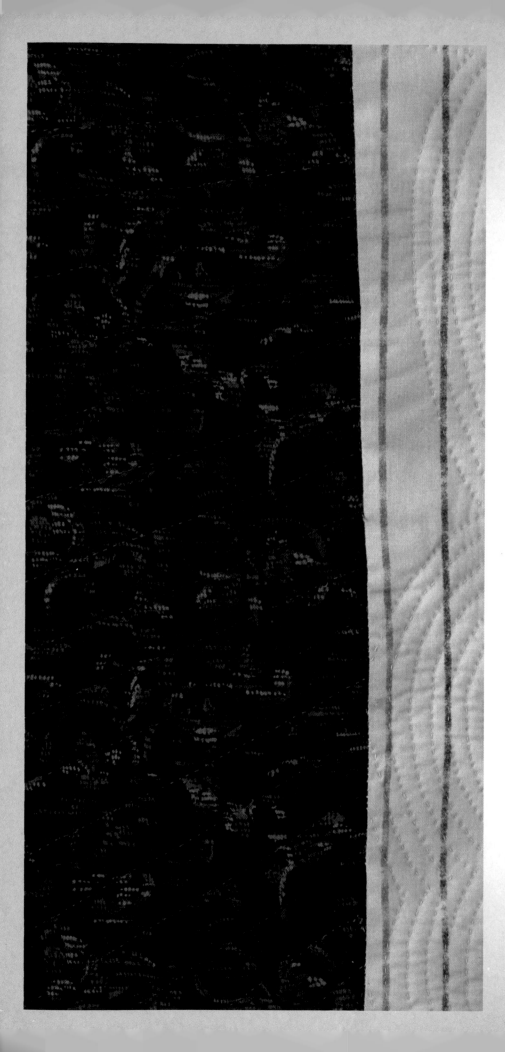

Assembling the Top

- When the appliqué is finished, trim the background to 35 1/2" x 46 1/2".
- For the 2 sides, cut borders 5 1/2" x 46 1/2".
- Following the corner pattern on page 87, cut 4 corners plus seam allowances. Sew these 4 corners on to the top and bottom of each of these 2 sides.
- Following the pattern for the rounded corners, trim the corners of the background fabric. Be sure to add the seam allowance to this background.
- Sew these 2 side borders with the added corners on to the background. To make smooth rounded corners, mark the sewing line along the curves. Pin the sides onto the background and pin every inch along the curves. Carefully sew the sides and the border curves onto the background sides and curves.
- For the top and bottom, cut 2 borders 5 1/2" x 45 1/2". Sew these borders to the top and bottom of the top.

Finishing

After the borders are sewn on to the background, sandwich the top, batting and backing. This was quilted by hand, but could be done by machine if desired. I outlined all the letters and used echo quilting around each of the letters. Using the echo quilting, I did not have to mark the pattern. Bind with the border fabric.

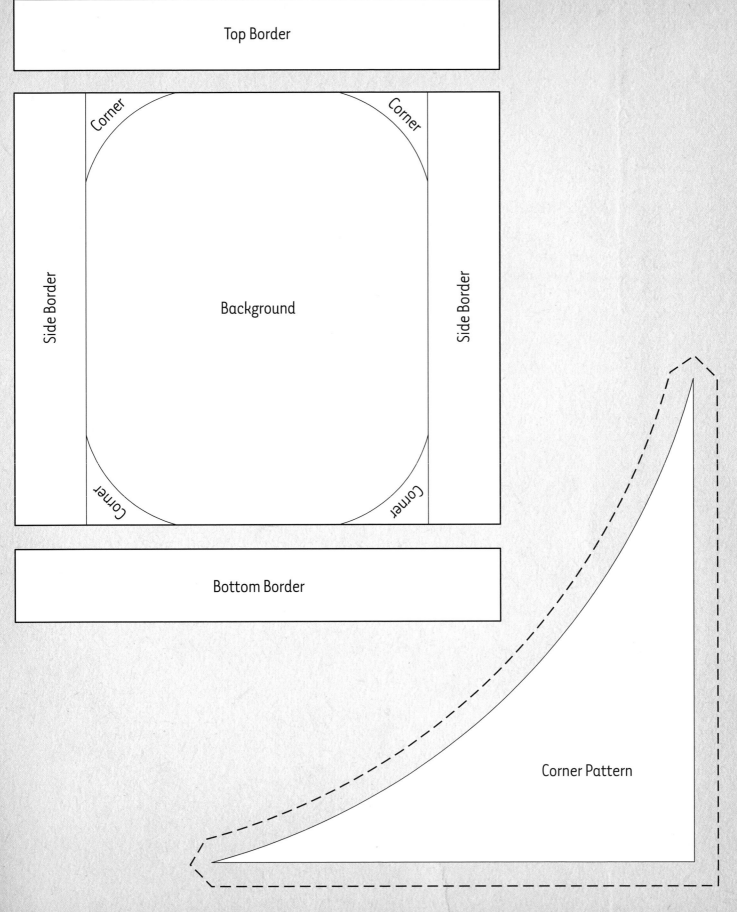

Top Border

Corner

Corner

Side Border

Background

Side Border

Corner

Corner

Bottom Border

Corner Pattern

Spencerian Alphabet
with Flowers

52" x 62"

This is another version of the Spencerian alphabet surrounded by a simple vine and flowers.
This version was done completely with fusible web and edged and quilted by machine.

Fabric Requirements

- Background – 2 1/2 yards
- Letters, outer border and binding – 2 yards
- Vine – 1/2 yard brown
- Flowers and leaves – scraps or fat quarters of green and flower colors of your choice

Cutting and Assembly

- Cut the background fabric to 36" x 46". This will be trimmed to the inside measurement of 34" x 44" after the appliqué is finished.
- Follow the instructions for applying the letters using the fusible web and fuse the web onto the letters.
- Before you fuse any of these letters in place on the background, lay the background on a flat surface and position the letters in an arrangement that is pleasing to you. I started the top row of A, B and C in the center and on the right side. The next 4 rows each contain 5 letters and I positioned the X, Y, and Z on the left side of the bottom row. This gave me an extra area on the top and bottom rows of letters to add the vine and flowers. When all the letters are in place, fuse them on to the background. Stitch around each letter with a decorative stitch for a finished look. I used a blanket stitch with #30 weight thread that matched the letters or flowers.

Borders

- Trim the background to 34 1/2" x 44 1/2".
- From the background fabric, cut 2 borders 8 1/2" x 44 1/2" and sew to the sides.
- Cut 2 borders 8 1/2" x 50 1/2" and sew to the top and bottom.
- For the vine, fuse about 1/2 yard of brown fabric onto fusible web. Cut a free form meandering vine 1/2" wide and fuse on to the 8" border. Fill in the areas of the top and bottom rows with a small piece of vine. Do not worry about piecing this vine as the flowers will cover these raw edges. This vine is approximately 200" long.
- There are 2 different flower sizes and 7 different leaf shapes. Position and fuse these leaves and the flowers along the vine as you wish, covering any raw edges of the vine where it was pieced.
- After the vine, the leaves and the flowers are fused, stitch around each for a finished look.
- Using the fabric of the letters, add a 1" border.

Finishing

- Mark the quilting design. Sandwich the top, batting and backing. This was quilted in a straight line diagonal pattern by machine. Bind with the outer border fabric.

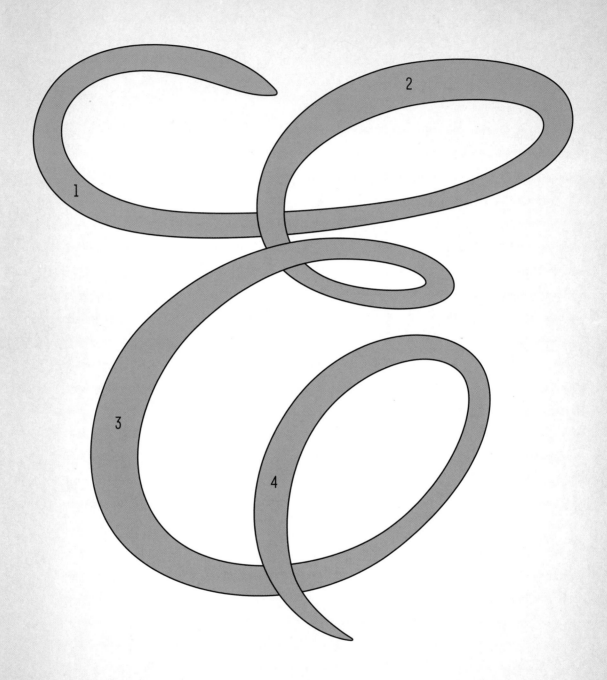

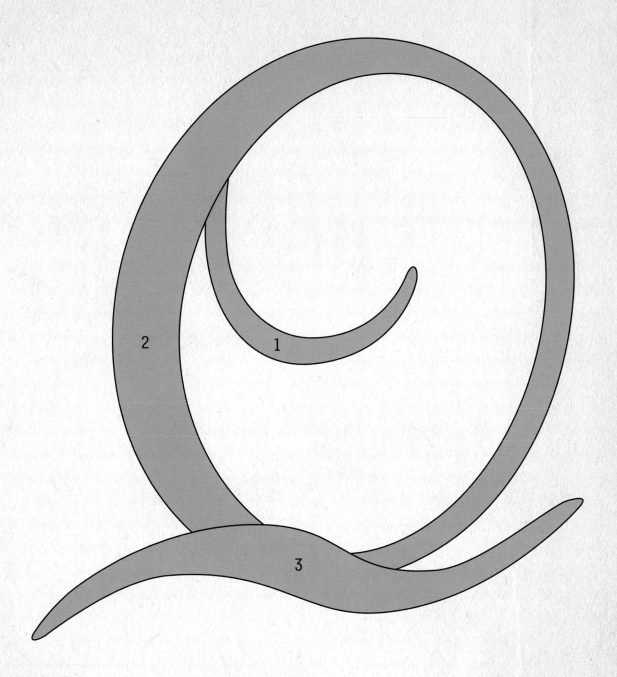

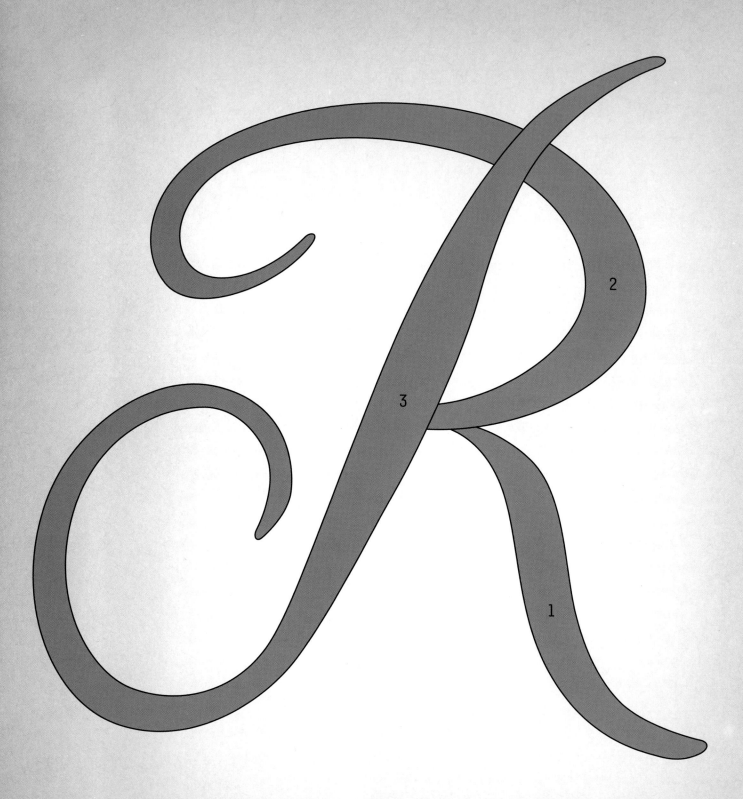

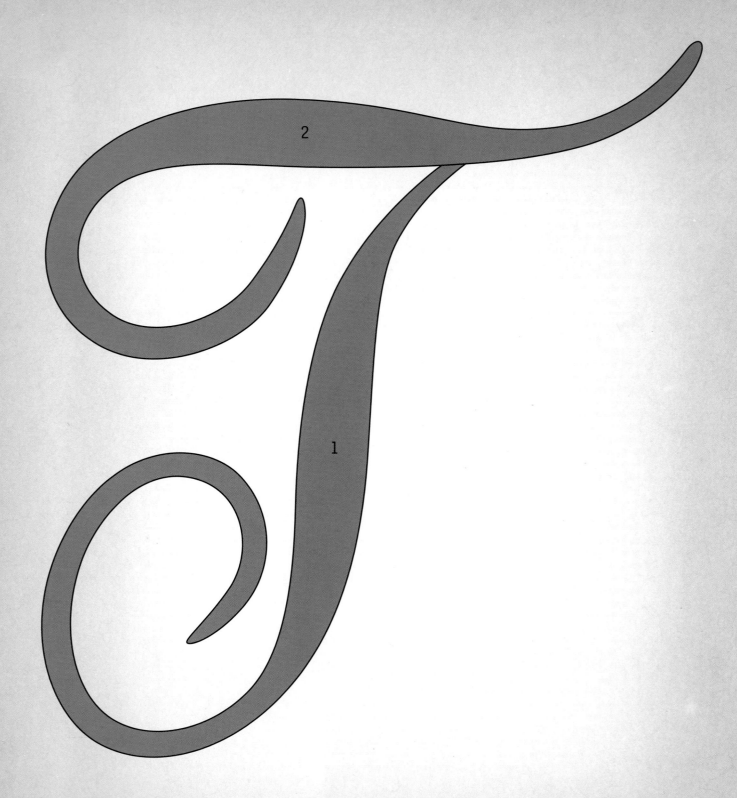

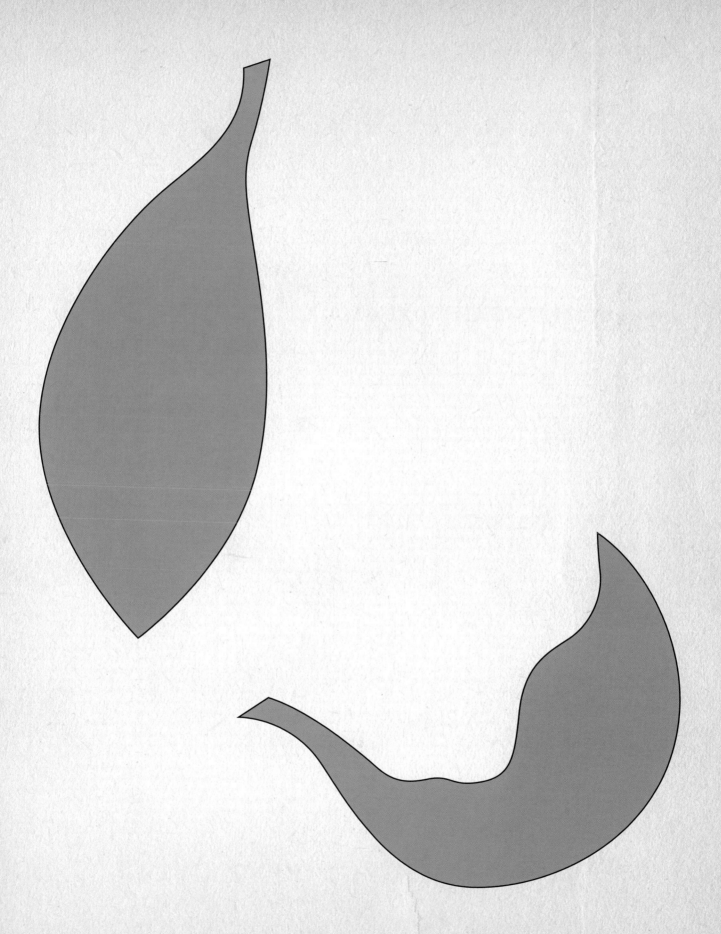

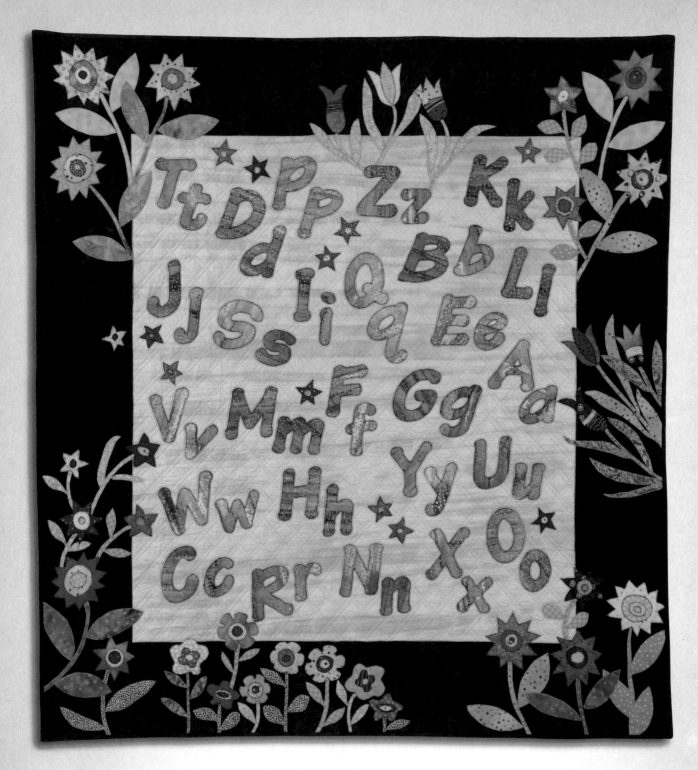

Gallery

Bea created a series of alphabet quilts for members of her family as she developed the patterns for this book. She has given most of them away, but some are pictured here.

This quilt features letters from the cursive alphabet, pages 34-46. She designed flowers especially for the border of this quilt.

Bea made the two blocks on this page for her own name. The top block features a Spencerian B (see page 91) and the bottom block features the floral B (page 59).

This very special
alphabet book was
made for Bea's great
granddaughter Lillie
Thomasset of Overland
Park, Kansas. Bea used
the letters from the
block alphabet (pages
12-17) and designs found
on pages 47-53 with a
zipper thrown in for fun.

Other Star Books